Baby Kangaroos

by Bob Dannon

![Houghton Mifflin Harcourt logo] **HOUGHTON MIFFLIN HARCOURT**
School Publishers

PHOTOGRAPHY CREDITS: Cover © Brakefield Photo; 1 © Biosphoto/Ruoso Cyril/Peter;
2 © Jochen Schlenker/Radius Images; 3 © Mitsuaki Iwago/Minden Pictures; 4 © Mitsuaki Iwago/Minden Pictures;
5 © Biosphoto/Ruoso Cyril/Peter; 6 © David Maitland/Getty Images; 7 © Brakefield Photo; 8 © Rosenfeld/Corbis;
9 © Jason Edwards/National Geographic/Getty Images; 10 © Peter Fakler/Alamy

Copyright © by Houghton Mifflin Harcourt Publishing Company

All rights reserved. No part of this work may be reproduced or transmitted in any form or by any means, electronic or
mechanical, including photocopying or recording, or by any information storage and retrieval system, without the prior
written permission of the copyright owner unless such copying is expressly permitted by federal copyright law. Requests
for permission to make copies of any part of the work should be addressed to Houghton Mifflin Harcourt School Publishers,
Attn: Permissions, 6277 Sea Harbor Drive, Orlando, Florida 32887-6777.

Printed in USA

ISBN-13: 978-0-547-02872-9
ISBN-10: 0-547-02872-5

10 11 12 1083 18 17 16 15 14
4500472120

If you have received these materials as examination copies free of charge, Houghton Mifflin Harcourt School Publishers
retains title to the materials and they may not be resold. Resale of examination copies is strictly prohibited.

Possession of this publication in print format does not entitle users to convert this publication, or any portion of it, into
electronic format.

Kangaroos live in Australia.
Every mother kangaroo has
a pouch.
The pouch is like a pocket
on her body.
A baby kangaroo stays inside its
mother's pouch for the first few
months of its life.

Baby Kangaroos

A young kangaroo is called
a joey.
A joey crawls right into its
mother's pouch after it is born.
The joey cannot see or hear.
It is as small as a fingernail.

The First Few Months
The pouch protects the joey.
It keeps the joey warm and cozy.
The joey grows inside the pouch.
After a few months,
it has ears, legs, and fur.

Leaving the Pouch

When the joey gets bigger, it begins to move around.

After six to eight months, the joey can leave the pouch for a few minutes.

Then it climbs back into the pouch.

Learning How to Hop

The joey keeps growing.
The joey follows its mother.
It learns to hop.

The joey returns to the pouch when
it gets scared or wants to rest.
Sometimes a mother kangaroo has
another baby.
Then the big joey shares the pouch
with its tiny brother or sister.

Growing Up

A joey drinks milk from its mother's pouch until it is about a year old.

Then the big joey can find its own food.

It is now as big as an adult.

Some girl kangaroos stay with
their mothers.
When they have joeys of their
own, the big family lives together.

Most boy kangaroos leave their
mothers.
They look for other kangaroos.
They start a new family.

Responding

How does a mother kangaroo's pouch help her joey? Make a chart and list three ways.

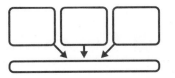

✎ **Write About It**

Text to World Draw a picture of a joey and its mother. Write a sentence about the joey.

✔ **WORDS TO KNOW**

baby	**learning**
begins	**until**
eight	**years**
follow	**young**

✔ **TARGET SKILL** **Conclusions**

Use details to figure out more about the text.

✔ **TARGET STRATEGY** **Visualize**

Picture what is happening as you read.

GENRE Informational text gives facts about a topic.